Introduction

If the words "pot holders" bring to mind a drawerful of thick grubby rags, then you need to try some of these fun pot holder patterns! They are quick and easy projects that are decorative but practical too. They can be personalized with your favorite fabrics and colors, and they make great gifts. This book offers 20 different patterns that cover a year of seasons and holidays. Several are based on traditional quilt-block patterns, some are pieced and some appliquéd. I hope you enjoy making these quick projects to spruce up your kitchen all year round!

Meet the Designer

Chris Malone has been sewing and crafting most of her life. As an accomplished sewist, quilter and designer, she has had hundreds of designs published in sewing and quilting publications and has authored several books of her own.

She is a regular contributor to *Quilter's World* magazine and Annie's quilting and sewing book titles. Chris' whimsical style has been a favorite of many quilters and sewists, and is easily recognizable at a glance.

Chris resides in the diverse and beautiful Willamette Valley of Oregon.

Table of Contents

General Instructions

The 20 pot holder designs in this book are all easy and fun projects that require a minimum of materials. Here are a few tips on the supplies you will need, general assembly instructions and finishing tips you may find helpful.

Basic Tools & Supplies

- Scissors for paper and fabric
- Rotary cutter, ruler and mat (optional)
- Nonpermanent (water- and/or air-soluble) fabric-marking tools
- Template material
- Sewing machine
- Walking or even-feed foot (optional)
- Hand-sewing needles
- Straight pins and pincushion
- Binding clips (optional)
- Seam ripper
- Steam/dry iron and ironing surface

Fabric

Use all-cotton fabrics for the projects in this book. Synthetic fabrics such as polyester and nylon can melt and burn easily. The fabric yardage requirements are small—these pot holders are a great way to use up scraps and fat quarters.

Batting

Layers of both 100 percent cotton batting and needle-punched insulated batting are used in most of the projects in this book. The cotton batting is soft and dense and won't melt from high heat. The insulated batting is added to reflect the heat back to the source. This breathable material has deep fibers that prevent conduction and a reflective metalized film that prevents radiant energy from passing through. **Do not add this batting to anything you will be using in the microwave.** Substitute a second layer of cotton batting in place of the insulated batting if you wish to use your pot holder in the microwave.

Walking or Even-Feed Foot

This sewing-machine foot is useful because a pot holder has multiple layers. Known as a walking or even-feed foot, it feeds the upper and lower layers of fabric and batting through the machine at the same rate to prevent wrinkles and folds.

General Assembly Instructions

Read all instructions carefully before beginning each project.

All seams are ¼" unless otherwise directed.

The finished measurements given for each project include the outer seam allowance.

Press each seam as you sew.

Appliqué

Many of the pot holders are made with appliqués using fusible web with paper release and a machine blanket stitch to finish the raw edges. Refer to Raw-Edge Fusible Appliqué on page 4 for specifics. Other appliqué methods may be substituted if desired. All of the appliqué patterns are reversed so they will face the correct direction when fused to the background. When appliqués overlap, slip the edge of one under the other before fusing.

Raw-Edge Fusible Appliqué

One of the easiest ways to appliqué is the raw-edge fusible-web method. Paper-backed fusible web individual pieces are fused to the wrong side of specified fabrics, cut out and then fused together in a motif or individually to a foundation fabric, where they are machine-stitched in place.

Choosing Appliqué Fabrics

Depending on the appliqué, you may want to consider using batiks. Batik is a much tighter weave and, because of the manufacturing process, does not fray. If you are thinking about using regular quilting cottons, be sure to stitch your raw-edge appliqués with blanket/buttonhole stitches instead of a straight stitch.

Cutting Appliqué Pieces

1. Fusible appliqué shapes should be reversed for this technique.

2. Trace the appliqué shapes onto the paper side of paper-backed fusible web. Leave at least ¼" between shapes. Cut out shapes leaving a margin around traced lines. **Note:** *If doing several identical appliqués, trace reversed shapes onto template material to make reusable templates for tracing shapes onto the fusible web.*

3. Follow manufacturer's instructions and fuse shapes to wrong side of fabric as indicated on pattern for color and number to cut.

4. Cut out appliqué shapes on traced lines. Remove paper backing from shapes.

5. Again following fusible web manufacturer's instructions, arrange and fuse pieces to quilt referring to quilt pattern. Or fuse together shapes on top of an appliqué ironing mat to make an appliqué motif that can then be fused to the quilt.

Stitching Appliqué Edges

Machine-stitch appliqué edges to secure the appliqués in place and help finish the raw edges with matching or invisible thread (Photo 1). **Note:** *To show stitching, all samples have been stitched with contrasting thread.*

Straight stitch

Buttonhole or blanket stitch

Photo 1

Invisible thread can be used to stitch appliqués down when using the blanket or straight stitches. Do not use it for the satin stitch. Definitely practice with invisible thread before using it on your quilt; it can sometimes be difficult to work with.

A short, narrow buttonhole or blanket stitch is most commonly used (Photo 2). Your machine manual may also refer to this as an appliqué stitch. Be sure to stitch next to the appliqué edge with the stitch catching the appliqué.

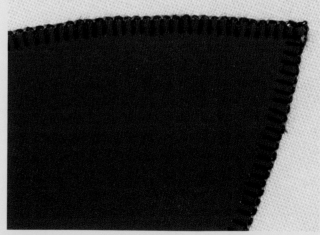

Photo 2

Practice turning inside and outside corners on scrap fabric before stitching appliqué pieces. Learn how your machine stitches so that you can make the pivot points smooth.

1. To stitch outer corners, stitch to the edge of the corner and stop with needle in the fabric at the corner point. Pivot to the next side of the corner and continue to sew (Photo 3). You will get a box on an outside corner.

Photo 3

2. To stitch inner corners, pivot at the inner point with needle in fabric (Photo 4). You will see a Y shape in the corner.

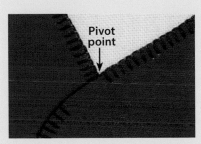

Pivot point

Photo 4

3. You can also use a machine straight stitch. Turn corners in the same manner, stitching to the corners and pivoting with needle in down position (Photo 5).

Photo 5

General Appliqué Tips

1. Use a light- to medium-weight stabilizer behind an appliqué to keep the fabric from puckering during machine stitching (Photo 6).

Photo 6

2. To reduce the stiffness of a finished appliqué, cut out the center of the fusible web shape, leaving ¼"–½" inside the pattern line. This gives a border of adhesive to fuse to the background and leaves the center soft and easy to quilt.

3. If an appliqué fabric is so light colored or thin that the background fabric shows through, fuse a lightweight interfacing to the wrong side of the fabric. You can also fuse a piece of the appliqué fabric to a matching piece, wrong sides together, and then apply the fusible with a drawn pattern to one side.

Appliqué continued

To add dimension to appliqué pieces, use the padded appliqué method, a technique in which batting is sewn into the appliqué shape. Refer to Padded Appliqué for specifics on using this method.

Padded Appliqué

Some of the projects are finished with a "padded" appliqué. In this technique, an appliqué piece is sewn with two layers of fabric and a layer of batting and then turned right side out through an opening. Padded appliqué gives dimensional interest to a project. Refer to General Instructions on page 3 for details about preparing templates from patterns.

1. Prepare template using pattern provided and trace the shape on the wrong side of the selected fabric. Fold the fabric in half with the right sides facing and the traced shape on top.

2. Pin this fabric to a scrap of batting that is slightly larger than traced shape and then sew on the traced lines as shown in Figure A.

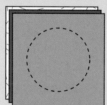

Figure A

3. The instructions will tell you whether you should leave a side opening for turning in the seam allowance, or if you should sew all around and then make a slash in one layer of fabric only for turning.

4. Cut out the shape ⅛"–¼" from the seam line, clip curves generously (or use pinking shears to cut out).

5. To make a slash, pinch the top layer of fabric and pull away that layer from the other fabric layer; make a little snip in the pinched fabric. Insert scissor tips into the hole and cut the fabric just enough to turn the shape right side out (Figure B). If desired, add a little no-fray solution to the cut edges of the slash and let it dry.

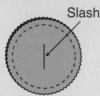

Figure B

6. After turning the shape right side out through the slash or side opening, whipstitch the cut edges of slash back together as shown in Figure C or slipstitch the side opening closed. Press the shape from the top side so it is flat and smooth at the edges.

Figure C

Binding

Many of the pot holder designs are finished with a binding on the raw edges. The individual instructions give the cutting width and number of strips needed to prepare straight-grain binding and, for curved edges, will specify the cutting width and length needed for bias binding. The bindings are prepared as double-fold for longevity.

Mitered Corner Binding

To give your quilts a professional finish, bindings need to be smooth and fit snugly over the edges of the quilt, be invisibly hand-stitched to the back of the quilt and have mitered corners that lie flat without gaps. With a little practice, you can complete mitered-corner bindings that any quilter will smile about.

1. Join binding strips on short ends with diagonal seams to make one long strip; trim seams to ¼" and press seams open (Figure A).

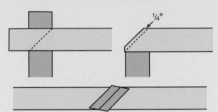

Figure A

2. Fold 1" of one short end to wrong side and press. Fold the binding strip in half with wrong sides together along length, referring to Figure B; press.

Figure B

3. Starting about 3" from the folded short end, sew binding to quilt top edges, matching raw edges and using a ¼" seam. Stop stitching ¼" from corner and backstitch (Figure C). Clip thread.

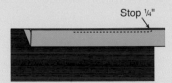

Figure C

4. Fold binding up at a 45-degree angle to seam and then down even with quilt edges, forming a pleat at corner, referring to Figure D. Take a stitch or two in the fold to hold the corner down.

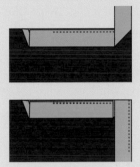

Figure D

5. Resume stitching from corner edge as shown in Figure D, down quilt side, backstitching ¼" from next corner. Repeat stitching to within 3" of starting point, and mitering all corners.

6. Trim binding end long enough to tuck inside starting end and complete stitching (Figure E).

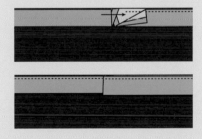

Figure E

7. Fold binding to quilt back, making sure that binding is pulled snugly against quilt raw edges and covering the stitching. Stitch in place by hand or machine to complete your quilt.

Cutting Bias Strips

Bias strips are cut at a 45-degree angle to the crosswise or lengthwise grain of the fabric. Strips cut on the bias will have stretch, which allows them to be used for appliqué and other applications where curving the strip is required, such as wrapping cord or binding rounded corners and projects. However, bias strips require careful handling to be sure the strips are not stretched out of shape or distorted.

1. Since bias strips are being cut from a square on the straight of grain, it is essential to know the length of continuous bias strips that can be cut from the square. To determine this length, first find the area of the square by multiplying the square's measurement by itself, then divide by the desired width of the strip.

For example, to find the total length of 2½"-wide bias that can be cut from a 12" square, multiply 12" x 12", which equals 144" and then divide 144" by 2½" to equal 57". This formula has been used to fill in the chart below for use as an easy reference.

2. Based on your project, determine the length and width of bias desired. Cut the size square needed along the straight grain referring to your chart. Place the 45-degree line on your ruler along the bottom edge of the square and cut diagonally across the square from corner to corner (Figure A).

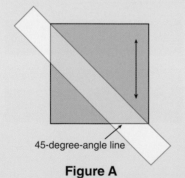

45-degree-angle line

Figure A

3. Being careful not to stretch the edge, place the ruler along the cut edge at the width desired and cut a strip (Figure B).

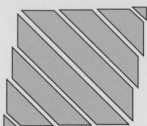

2½"

Figure B

4. Continue cutting strips, being careful with the bias edges, until the square is completely cut (Figure C).

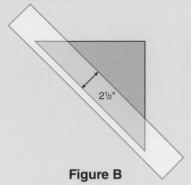

Figure C

5. Position and pin strips perpendicular to each other with right sides together. Join the strips with 45-degree diagonal seams for a continuous strip (Figure D1). Trim seams to ¼", then press seams open and trim dog ears (Figure D2).

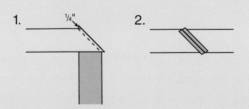

1.   ¼"   2.

Figure D

	BIAS WIDTH	1"	1¼"	1½"	1¾"	2"	2¼"	2¼"
SQUARE SIZE	12" square	144"	115"	96"	82"	72"	64"	57"
	18" square	324"	259"	216"	185"	162"	144"	129"
	27" square	729"	583"	486"	416"	364"	324"	291"
	36" square	1,296"	1,036"	864"	740"	648"	576"	518"

Continuous Bias Chart

Hangers

To hang a pot holder on the wall, you can make a matching-fabric or ribbon hanging loop by stitching it into the binding seam, or you can sew one or two plastic rings to the back. The rings can be hand sewn on just one corner or sewn to each top corner to hang the pot holder like a mini quilt.

For a fabric hanging loop, cut the fabric to the size indicated in the instructions. Fold the strip in half lengthwise, wrong sides together and press. Open the strip and fold in each long edge almost to the fold line and press. Refold in the center and topstitch close to the long folded edges as shown in Figure 1. Attach the hanging loop to the pot holder as directed in individual instructions.

Figure 1

For plastic rings, position the ring(s) on pot holder top back corner(s) and hand-stitch in place as shown in Figure 2, being careful not to stitch through the front of the pot holder. ●

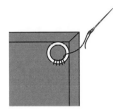

Figure 2

Patchwork Valentine

Whether it's a gift for a special valentine or just to express your love of cooking, this heart-shaped pot holder fits the bill. Dig out your red or pink scraps and whip it up for a quick project.

Skill Level
Beginner

Specifications
Pot Holder Size: 8½" x 7½" excluding loop

Materials
- Scraps assorted red or pink fabrics
- Fat quarter red tonal
- 1 (8") square cotton batting
- 1 (8") square needle-punched insulated batting
- Thread
- Basic sewing tools and supplies

Project Notes
Read all instructions before beginning this project.

Stitch right sides together using a ¼" seam allowance unless otherwise specified.

Refer to General Instructions on page 3 for specific construction and appliqué tips and techniques.

Cutting

From assorted red or pink scraps:
- Cut 21 (2") A squares and 1 (1¼" x 5") strip for hanging loop.

From red tonal:
- Cut 1 (8") backing square.

Completing the Pot Holder
Refer to the Placement Diagram and project photo throughout for positioning of pieces.

1. Arrange six A squares into two rows of three squares each as shown in Figure 1. Sew the squares together in each row; press. Sew the rows together; press.

Figure 1

2. Referring to Figure 2, arrange remaining 15 A squares into three rows of five squares each. Sew the squares together in each row; press. Sew the rows together; press.

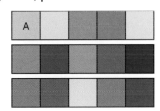

Figure 2

3. Sew the smaller unit to the top right side of the larger unit, matching seams and side edges; press seam toward smaller unit.

4. To shape heart, draw a line from seam to seam on four corners as shown in Figure 3. Cut on the drawn lines.

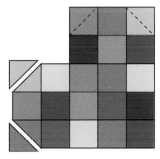

Figure 3

5. Referring to General Instructions on page 9, prepare hanging loop. Fold loop in half and pin raw edges to the upper square of heart on right side as shown in Figure 4. Baste to secure.

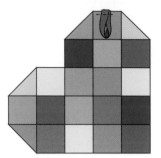

Figure 4

6. Layer pieces as follows: cotton batting square; insulated batting square, shiny side up; backing square, right side up; and heart-shaped front, centered with right side down. Pin layers to secure. Following outside edge of heart-shaped front, sew around edges, leaving a 3½" opening in one straight side. Trim battings and backing to match front. To reduce bulk, trim insulated batting close to seam. Trim corners and turn right side out. Fold in seam

allowance of opening and slip-stitch closed. Press edges flat and smooth.

7. Topstitch ¼" from outside edge and ¼" from inner squares or quilt as desired to finish. ●

Patchwork Valentine
Placement Diagram 8½" x 7½"
excluding loop

Sunny Side Up

Breakfast will be more fun when you use this whimsical chicken pot holder! It has an appliquéd beak, dimensional wings and feet, and the comb doubles as a hanger.

Skill Level
Beginner

Specifications
Pot Holder Size: 8" x 8¾" excluding loops, wings and feet

Materials
- Scraps black egg print, gold tonal and red-with-white dot
- Fat quarter white chicken-wire print
- 1 each 9" x 9¾", 5" x 11" and 3" x 10" rectangle cotton batting
- 1 (9" x 9¾") rectangle needle-punched insulated batting
- Thread
- 2 (½") black buttons
- Fusible web with paper release
- Basic sewing tools and supplies

Project Notes
Read all instructions before beginning this project.

Stitch right sides together using a ¼" seam allowance unless otherwise specified.

Refer to General Instructions on page 3 for specific construction and appliqué tips and techniques.

Cutting
Prepare body template using pattern provided on insert.

From red-with-white dot:
- Cut 1 (1¾" x 5") and 2 (1¾" x 3") strips for hanging loops.

From white chicken-wire print:
- Cut 2 body shapes using prepared template.

From each 9 x 9¾" batting rectangle:
- Cut 1 body shape using prepared template.

Completing the Pot Holder
Refer to the Placement Diagram and project photo throughout for positioning of pieces.

1. Baste cotton batting body to wrong side of one fabric body shape for pot holder front.

2. Referring to Raw-Edge Fusible Appliqué on page 4, prepare appliqué templates using beak pattern provided on the insert for this pot holder.

3. Trace appliqué shapes onto paper side of fusible web referring to list below for number to trace and cut out. Apply shapes to wrong side of fabric as listed below.

Gold tonal: 1 beak

4. Cut out appliqué shape and remove paper backing. Place beak on the pot holder front referring to Figure 1. Fuse in place.

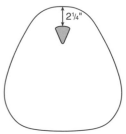

Figure 1

5. Machine blanket-stitch around beak using matching thread.

6. Make foot template using pattern provided on insert. Referring to Padded Appliqué on page 6, prepare two feet from gold tonal, using 3" x 10" cotton batting rectangle and leaving top edge open for turning.

7. Quilt each foot by stitching down the center and then branch out toward the toes as shown in Figure 2.

Figure 2

8. Referring to Figure 3, pin feet to bottom edge of pot holder front with feet ⅞" apart and raw edges aligned. Baste to hold.

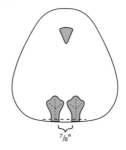

Figure 3   **Figure 4**

9. Referring to General Instructions on page 9, prepare three hanging loops. Fold each loop in half and, with longer loop in center, pin ends to top center of pot holder front as shown in Figure 4. Baste to secure.

10. Layer pot holder front and backing with right sides together on the insulated batting body, shiny side down; pin layers to secure. Sew around edges, leaving a 3½" opening in one side. To reduce bulk, trim insulated batting close to seam. Clip curves and turn right side out. Fold in seam allowance of opening and slip-stitch closed. Press edges flat and smooth.

11. Topstitch ¼" from outside edge and quilt around beak appliqué.

12. Make wing template using pattern provided. Referring to Padded Appliqué on page 6, prepare two wings from black egg print, using the 5" x 11" cotton batting rectangle and making a 1" slash for turning.

13. Topstitch ¼" from outside edge of each wing.

14. Position wings on pot holder front 4" down from top of head and 2¾" in from sides as shown in Figure 5. Sew over previous topstitching lines where wings overlap pot holder front to attach.

15. Sew black buttons to the face for eyes to finish. ●

Figure 5

Sunny Side Up
Placement Diagram 8" x 8¾"
excluding loops, wings & feet

Lamb Chops

This cute lamb pot holder is quick and easy to make and practical to use. He has an appliquéd face and dangling legs with a hanging loop for a tail.

Skill Level

Beginner

Specifications

Pot Holder Size: 8" x 8¾" excluding loop and legs

Materials

- Scraps black tonal, black solid and white tonal
- Fat quarter gray-with-white dot
- 1 each 9" x 9¾" and 4" x 10" rectangle cotton batting
- 1 (9" x 9¾") rectangle needle-punched insulated batting
- Thread
- 2 (½") black buttons
- Fusible web with paper release
- Basic sewing tools and supplies

Project Notes

Read all instructions before beginning this project.

Stitch right sides together using a ¼" seam allowance unless otherwise specified.

Refer to General Instructions on page 3 for specific construction and appliqué tips and techniques.

Cutting

Prepare body template using pattern provided on insert.

From black tonal:

- Cut 1 (1¾" x 5") strip for hanging loop.

From gray-with-white dot:

- Cut 2 body shapes using prepared template.

From each 9 x 9¾" batting rectangle:

- Cut 1 body shape using prepared template.

Completing the Pot Holder

Refer to the Placement Diagram and project photo throughout for positioning of pieces.

1. Baste cotton batting body to wrong side of one fabric body shape for pot holder front.

2. Referring to Raw-Edge Fusible Appliqué on page 4, prepare appliqué templates using face, wooly cap and ear patterns provided on the insert for this pot holder.

3. Trace appliqué shapes onto paper side of fusible web referring to list below for number to trace and cut out. Apply shapes to wrong side of fabric as listed below.

- White tonal: 1 face
- Black tonal: 1 woolly cap
- Black solid: 2 ears (1 reversed)

4. Cut out appliqué shapes and remove paper backing. Place face appliqué on the pot holder front referring to Figure 1. Tuck ears under side of face and top with woolly cap. Fuse in place.

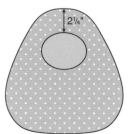

2¼"

Figure 1

5. Machine blanket-stitch around each appliqué using matching thread.

6. Make leg template using pattern provided on insert. Referring to Padded Appliqué on page 6, prepare two legs from black solid, using the 4" x 10" cotton batting rectangle and leaving the top edge open for turning.

7. Stitch a curved line to mark hooves on each leg as shown in Figure 2.

Figure 2

8. Referring to Figure 3, pin legs to bottom edge of pot holder front with legs ½" apart and raw edges aligned. Baste to hold.

½"

Figure 3

9. Referring to General Instructions on page 9, prepare the hanging loop. Fold loop in half and pin ends to top center of body front, again referring to Figure 3. Baste to secure.

10. Layer pot holder front and backing with right sides together on the insulated batting body, shiny side down; pin layers to secure. Sew around edges, leaving a 3½" opening in one side. To reduce bulk, trim insulated batting close to seam. Clip curves and turn right side out. Fold in seam allowance of opening and slip-stitch closed. Press edges flat and smooth.

11. Topstitch ¼" from outside edge and quilt around each appliqué.

12. Sew black buttons to the face for eyes to finish. ●

Lamb Chops
Placement Diagram 8" x 8¾"
excluding loop & legs

Riblets

Every kitchen needs a pink polka-dot pig! This pot holder uses the same body pattern as the lamb and chicken, and the three barnyard characters make an adorable set.

Skill Level
Beginner

Specifications
Pot Holder Size: 8" x 8¾" excluding loop and hooves

Materials
- Scraps dark and light pink tonals and black tonal
- Fat quarter white-with-pink dot
- Cotton batting
- 1 (9" x 9¾") rectangle needle-punched insulated batting
- Thread
- 2 (⅜") light pink buttons
- 2 (½") black buttons
- Fusible web with paper release
- Basic sewing tools and supplies

Project Notes
Read all instructions before beginning this project.

Stitch right sides together using a ¼" seam allowance unless otherwise specified.

Refer to General Instructions on page 3 for specific construction and appliqué tips and techniques.

Cutting
Prepare body template using pattern provided on insert.

From dark pink tonal:
- Cut 1 (1¾" x 5") strip for hanging loop.

From white-with-pink dot:
- Cut 2 body shapes using prepared template.

From cotton batting:
- Cut 1 (2" x 12") rectangle and 1 body shape using prepared template.

From insulated batting:
- Cut 1 body shape using prepared template.

Completing the Pot Holder

Refer to the Placement Diagram and project photo throughout for positioning of pieces.

1. Baste cotton batting body to wrong side of one fabric body piece for pot holder front.

2. Referring to Raw-Edge Fusible Appliqué on page 4, prepare appliqué templates using face, snout and ear patterns provided on the insert for this pot holder.

3. Trace appliqué shapes onto paper side of fusible web referring to list below for number to trace and cut out. Apply shapes to wrong side of fabric as listed below.

- Dark pink tonal: 1 face
- Light pink tonal: 1 snout and 2 ears

4. Cut out appliqué shapes and remove paper backing. Place face appliqué on the pot holder front referring to Figure 1. Tuck ears under top of face and add snout. Fuse in place.

Figure 1

5. Machine blanket-stitch around each appliqué using matching thread.

6. Make hoof template using pattern provided. Referring to Padded Appliqué on page 6, prepare two hooves from black tonal, using the 2" x 12" cotton batting rectangle and leaving the straight top edge open for turning.

7. Stitch three lines down each hoof as shown in Figure 2.

Figure 2

8. Referring to Figure 3, pin hooves to bottom edge of pot holder front with hooves ¾" apart and raw edges aligned. Baste to hold.

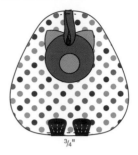

Figure 3

9. Referring to General Instructions on page 9, prepare the hanging loop. Fold loop in half and pin ends to top center of body front, again referring to Figure 3. Baste to secure.

10. Layer pot holder front on the pot holder back with right sides together; place on the insulated batting square, shiny side up. Pin layers to secure. Sew around edges, leaving a 3½" opening in one side. To reduce bulk, trim insulated batting close to seam. Clip curves and turn right side out. Fold in seam allowance of opening and slip-stitch closed. Press edges flat and smooth.

11. Topstitch ¼" from outside edge and quilt by stitching around each appliqué.

12. Sew black buttons to the face for eyes and pink buttons to snout to finish. ●

Riblets
Placement Diagram 8" x 8³⁄₄"
excluding loop & hooves

April Showers

We have to put up with a little rain sometimes if we want our flowers to bloom! This pot holder has a little pocket to slip your hand into and a perky umbrella appliqué on top.

Skill Level
Beginner

Specifications
Pot Holder Size: 8½" in diameter

Materials
- Scraps dark gray tonal and pink dot
- Fat quarter each light gray print, green print and pink tonal
- 2 (8½") squares cotton batting
- 1 (8½") square needle-punched insulated batting
- Thread
- 1 (¾") plastic ring
- Fusible web with paper release
- Basic sewing tools and supplies

Project Notes
Read all instructions before beginning this project.

Stitch right sides together using a ¼" seam allowance unless otherwise specified.

Refer to General Instructions on page 3 for specific construction and appliqué tips and techniques.

Cutting
Prepare templates for A Pocket and B Circle using patterns provided.

From light gray print:
- Cut 1 backing circle using prepared B template.
- Cut 2 pocket pieces using prepared A template.

From green print:
- Cut 1 B circle using prepared B template.

From pink tonal:
- Cut 2½"-wide bias strips to measure 40" when joined for binding.

Completing the Pot Holder
Refer to the Placement Diagram and project photo throughout for positioning of pieces.

1. Using the A Pocket template, trim one cotton batting square. Baste to wrong side of one pocket piece for pocket front.

2. Referring to Raw-Edge Fusible Appliqué on page 4, prepare appliqué templates using umbrella, umbrella cap and umbrella handle patterns provided on the insert for this pot holder.

3. Trace appliqué shapes onto paper side of fusible web referring to list below for number to trace and cut out. Apply shapes to wrong side of fabric as listed below.

- Dark gray tonal: 1 each umbrella handle and umbrella cap
- Pink dot: 1 umbrella

4. Cut out appliqué shapes and remove paper backing. Arrange appliqués on pocket front. Fuse in place.

5. Machine blanket-stitch around each appliqué using matching thread.

9. Layer the B circle, right side up; cotton batting circle; insulated batting circle, shiny side down; and backing circle, right side down. Pin layers to secure. Quilt a 2" grid to hold layers together.

10. Referring to Figure 2, position the pocket on the stitched B unit, securing the edges with pins or clips. Baste.

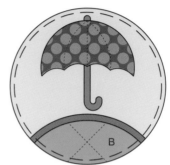

Figure 2

6. With wrong sides together, pin remaining pocket piece to the back of appliquéd pocket front; quilt around appliqués. Quilt spoke lines in the umbrella using dark pink thread to complete the pocket.

7. Referring to General Instructions on page 8, prepare bias binding strips. Bind bottom curved edge of the pocket as shown in Figure 1.

11. Referring to General Instructions on page 8, bind outside raw edges.

12. Referring to the General Instructions on page 9, sew the plastic ring to the back top center to finish. ●

Figure 1

8. Using the B Circle template, trim the remaining cotton batting square and the insulated batting square.

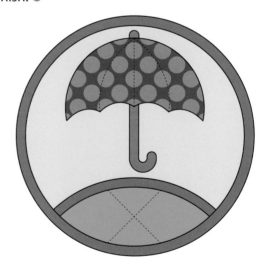

April Showers
Placement Diagram 8¹⁄₂" in diameter

May Flowers

After the April showers come the beautiful May flowers! This pot holder has a pocket for your hand and dimensional flowers in sweet spring colors.

Skill Level
Beginner

Specifications
Pot Holder Size: 7½" x 8½"

Materials
- Scraps green print, pink dot and pink tonal
- Fat quarter each white-with-green dot and pink-with-green dot
- ¼ yard green stripe
- Scraps cotton batting
- 1 (7½" x 8½") rectangle needle-punched insulated batting
- Thread
- 2 (⁷⁄₁₆") and 1 (⅝") white buttons
- White pearl cotton No. 8 or 12, or embroidery floss
- 2 (¾") plastic rings
- Fusible web with paper release
- Basic sewing tools and supplies

Project Notes
Read all instructions before beginning this project.

Stitch right sides together using a ¼" seam allowance unless otherwise specified.

Refer to General Instructions on page 3 for specific construction and appliqué tips and techniques.

Cutting

From green print:
- Cut 1 (1½" x 7½") A rectangle.

From white-with-green dot:
- Cut 1 each 5½" x 7½" B rectangle, 6½" x 7½" pocket lining and 7½" x 8½" pot holder backing.

From pink-with-green dot:
- Cut 1 (7½" x 8½") pot holder front.

From green stripe:
- Cut 2 (2½" by fabric width) binding strips.

From cotton batting:
- Cut 1 each 6½" x 7½" and 7½" x 8½" rectangle, and 3 (2½") squares.

Completing the Pot Holder
Refer to the Placement Diagram and project photo throughout for positioning of pieces.

1. Sew A and B together on long edges to make the pocket front; press seam open.

2. Baste the 6½" x 7½" cotton batting rectangle to wrong side of pocket front.

3. Referring to Raw-Edge Fusible Appliqué on page 4, prepare appliqué templates using leaf pattern provided on the insert for this pot holder.

4. Trace appliqué shape onto paper side of fusible web referring to list below for number to trace and cut out. Apply shapes to wrong side of fabric as listed below.

- Green print: 4 leaves and 2 (¼" x 2") and 1 (¼" x 3") stems

5. Cut out appliqué shapes and remove paper backing. Referring to Figure 1, arrange stem appliqués on pocket front with longer stem in center and a shorter stem on each side. Fuse in place. Add leaf appliqués.

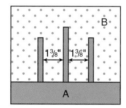

Figure 1

6. Machine blanket-stitch around each appliqué using matching thread.

7. Make large and small flower templates using patterns provided. Referring to Padded Appliqué on page 6, prepare one large flower from pink dot and two small flowers from pink tonal, using 2½" cotton batting squares and making a 1" slash for turning.

8. Using 1 strand of pearl cotton or 2 strands of floss, stitch a running stitch around the edges of each flower as shown in the photo on page 27.

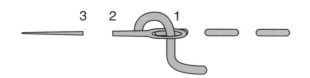

Running Stitch

9. Pin the appliquéd pocket front to the pocket lining, wrong sides together; stitch around each appliqué. Stitch a vein line in each leaf.

10. Sew the large white button to the center of the large flower, and then sew through the button to attach flower to the pocket, overlapping top of center stem. Repeat with the small white buttons and small flowers on the side stems.

11. Referring to General Instructions on page 8, prepare binding strips for double-fold binding. Apply to the top edge of the pocket.

12. Layer pot holder backing, right side down; insulated batting rectangle, shiny side down; the 7½" x 8½" cotton batting rectangle; and pot holder front, right side up. Pin layers to secure. Quilt a 2" diagonal grid to hold layers together.

13. Place the pocket right side up on top of the pot holder with side and bottom edges even; pin or clip to hold. Baste.

14. Referring to General Instructions on page 7, bind outside raw edges.

15. Sew a plastic ring to each back top corner to finish. ●

May Flowers
Placement Diagram 7½" x 8½"

Happy Camper

If your home is on the road as often as possible, you may need this pot holder! The curtained window, awning and door are appliquéd, and the tire is a dimensional embellishment.

Skill Level
Beginner

Specifications
Pot Holder Size: 9¼" x 7¼" excluding loop and tire

Materials
- Scraps dark gray and yellow tonals, salmon plaid, turquoise-with-orange dot and turquoise print
- Fat quarter white-with-gray grid
- ⅛ yard blue-with-gray plaid
- Scraps cotton batting
- 1 (8½" x 10½") rectangle needle-punched insulated batting
- Thread
- 1 (⅞") gray metal button
- 1 (⅜") yellow button
- Fusible web with paper release
- Basic sewing tools and supplies

Project Notes
Read all instructions before beginning this project.

Stitch right sides together using a ¼" seam allowance unless otherwise specified.

Refer to General Instructions on page 3 for specific construction and appliqué tips and techniques.

Cutting

From dark gray tonal:
- Cut 1 (1¼" x 5") strip for hanging loop.

From white-with-gray grid:
- Cut 2 (6½" x 10½") B rectangles.

From blue-with–gray plaid:
- Cut 1 (2¼" by fabric width) strips.
  Subcut strip into 2 (2¼" x 10½") A strips.

From cotton batting:
- Cut 1 (8½" x 10½") rectangle and 1 (3") square.

Completing the Pot Holder
Refer to the Placement Diagram and project photo throughout for positioning of pieces.

1. Sew one each A and B rectangle together on long sides to make an A-B unit as shown in Figure 1. Repeat to make a second A-B unit. Press seam on one unit toward A and seam on other unit toward B.

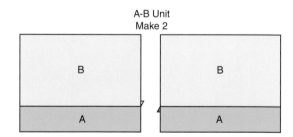

A-B Unit
Make 2

Figure 1

2. Prepare camper cutting template using pattern provided; use template to cut a camper front from one A-B unit, matching the seam to the line on the template. Reverse the template to cut the camper back from the second A-B unit. Use the template to cut the cotton and insulated batting pieces to size, trimming the insulated batting with shiny side down.

3. Center the camper front on cotton batting rectangle and baste edges.

4. Referring to Raw-Edge Fusible Appliqué on page 4, prepare appliqué templates using door window, door, window, curtain, doorstep and awning patterns provided on the insert for this pot holder.

5. Trace appliqué shapes onto paper side of fusible web referring to list below for number to trace and cut out. Apply shapes to wrong side of fabric as listed below.

- Dark gray tonal: 1 doorstep
- Yellow tonal: 1 each window and door window
- Salmon plaid: 1 door
- Turquoise-with-orange dot: 1 curtain
- Turquoise print: 1 awning

6. Cut out appliqué shapes and remove paper backing. Arrange appliqués on the camper front referring to Figure 2. Fuse in place.

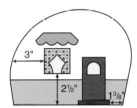

Figure 2

7. Machine blanket-stitch around each appliqué using matching thread.

8. Referring to General Instructions on page 9, prepare the hanging loop. Fold loop in half and pin ends to side of camper, matching raw edges as shown in Figure 3. Baste to secure.

Figure 3

9. Layer pot-holder front and back with right sides facing and seams matching on the insulated batting square, shiny side down; pin layers to secure. Sew around edges, leaving a 3½" opening in one side. Clip curves and turn right side out. Fold in seam allowance of opening and slip-stitch closed. Press edges flat and smooth.

10. Topstitch ¼" from outside edge and quilt by stitching around each appliqué.

11. Make tire template using pattern provided. Referring to Padded Appliqué on page 6, prepare one tire from dark gray tonal, using the 3" cotton batting square and making a 1" slash for turning. Topstitch ⅜" from edge.

12. Sew gray metal button to the center of the tire and then sew to camper near the bottom edge referring to the Placement Diagram. Sew the yellow button to the door for a doorknob to finish. ●

Happy Camper
Placement Diagram 9¼" x 7¼"
excluding loop & tire

Catch of the Day

If fishing is your hobby, or if fish is just a favorite dish, this would be a fun pot holder for your kitchen. The scallop-shape scales are dimensional and a button forms the eye.

Skill Level
Beginner

Specifications
Pot Holder Size: 9¾" x 8" excluding loop

Materials
- 5" x 12" rectangle blue tonal
- Fat quarter each blue print and turquoise tonal
- 1 each 10¼" x 8½" and 2" x 10" rectangle cotton batting
- 1 (10¼" x 8½") rectangle needle-punched insulated batting
- Thread
- 1 (¹¹⁄₁₆") turquoise button
- Fusible web with paper release
- Basic sewing tools and supplies

Project Notes
Read all instructions before beginning this project.

Stitch right sides together using a ¼" seam allowance unless otherwise specified.

Refer to General Instructions on page 3 for specific construction and appliqué tips and techniques.

Cutting

From blue tonal:
- Cut 1 (1¾" x 5") strip for hanging loop.

From blue print:
- Cut 2 (5½" x 8½") A rectangles.

From turquoise tonal:
- Cut 2 (6½" x 8½") B rectangles.

Completing the Pot Holder
Refer to the Placement Diagram and project photo throughout for positioning of pieces.

1. Make scallop template using pattern provided on insert. Referring to Padded Appliqué on page 6, prepare three scallops from blue tonal, using the 2" x 10" cotton batting rectangle and leaving straight top edge open for turning.

2. Topstitch ¼" from outer edge of each scallop.

3. Position the scallops along one long side of an A rectangle as shown in Figure 1, leaving ½" open at each end. Baste in place.

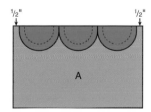

Figure 1

4. With right sides together, pin a B rectangle over scallop edge of A and stitch through all layers to make the pot holder front as shown in Figure 2; press seam toward B.

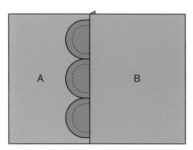

Figure 2

5. Stitch remaining A and B rectangles together to form pot holder back; press seam toward A.

6. Prepare body template using pattern provided on insert. Align seam line on template with seam on pot holder front, placing end labeled A on A piece and end labeled B on B piece; cut fish shape; repeat to cut pot holder back. Use template to cut one fish shape from each batting.

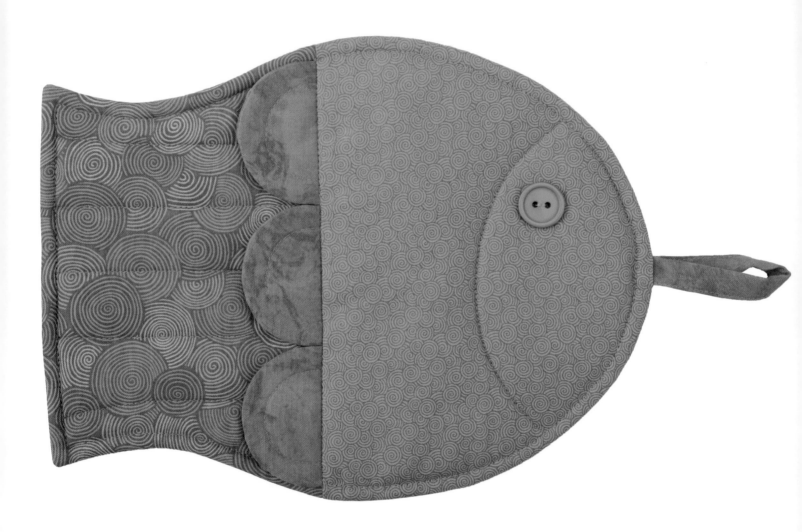

7. Referring to General Instructions on page 9, prepare hanging loop. Fold loop in half and pin to mouth end of pot holder front as shown in Figure 3. Baste to secure.

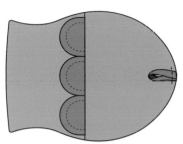

Figure 3

8. Layer and pin cotton batting; insulated batting, shiny side down; pot holder back, right side up; and pot holder front, right side down. Sew around edges, leaving a 3½" opening at tail end. To reduce bulk, trim insulated batting close to seam. Clip curves and turn right side out. Fold in seam allowance of opening and slip-stitch closed. Press edges flat and smooth.

9. Topstitch ¼" from outside edge, stitch in the ditch between A and B pieces and quilt a rounded shape to mark head area. Quilt lines down the tail.

10. Sew button to the head for eye to finish. ●

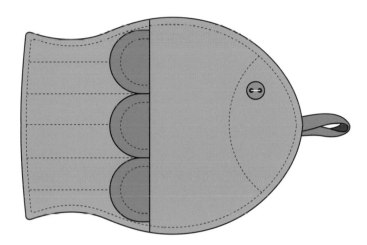

Catch of the Day
Placement Diagram 9¾" x 8"
excluding loop

Stars & Stripes

This pot holder has a pocket at each end so you can slip your hands inside to hold casseroles or baking pans. It makes a great hot pad to put in the center of the table too. The Wonky Star blocks, and red and white stripes will give an Americana look to the kitchen or patio.

Skill Level
Beginner

Specifications
Pot Holder Size: 27" x 8" excluding loops
Block Size: 7½" x 7½" finished
Number of Blocks: 2

Materials
- ¼ yard white tonal
- ⅜ yard red tonal
- ½ yard each gold and dark blue tonals
- Cotton batting
- 1 (10" x 29") rectangle needle-punched insulated batting
- Thread
- Basic sewing tools and supplies

Project Notes
Read all instructions before beginning this project.

Stitch right sides together using a ¼" seam allowance unless otherwise specified.

Refer to General Instructions on page 3 for specific construction and appliqué tips and techniques.

Cutting

From white tonal:
- Cut 2 (2" by fabric width) strips.
  Subcut strips into 2 (2" x 27") F strips.

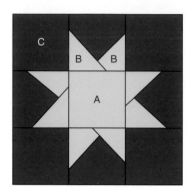

Wonky Star
7½" x 7½" Finished Block
Make 2

From red tonal:
- Cut 3 (2" by fabric width) strips.
  Subcut strips into 3 (2" x 27") E strips and 2 (1¾" x 5") strips for hanging loops.

From gold tonal:
- Cut 1 (10" by fabric width) strip.
  Subcut strip into 1 (10" x 29") backing rectangle, 2 (3") A squares and 8 (3") B squares. Cut the B squares in half on 1 diagonal to make 16 B triangles.

From dark blue tonal:
- Cut 1 (8" by fabric width) strip.
  Subcut strip into 2 (8") D squares and 16 (3") C squares.
- Cut 2 (2½" by fabric width) binding strips.

From cotton batting:
- Cut 1 (10" x 29") rectangle and 2 (8") squares.

Completing the Pot Holder

Refer to the Placement Diagram and project photo throughout for positioning of pieces.

1. Position a B triangle right sides together across one corner of a C square and sew ¼" from the edge of the B triangle as shown in Figure 1.

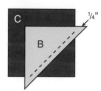

Figure 1

2. Trim the C corner even with the edge of B as shown in Figure 2. Press the B triangle open; trim excess B even with the edges of C, again referring to Figure 2.

Figure 2

3. Referring to Figure 3, repeat steps 1 and 2 to add a second B triangle to the adjacent corner of C to complete a point unit, changing position of B on C before sewing to vary height and angle of each point.

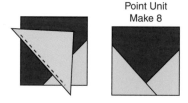

Figure 3

4. Repeat steps 1–3 to make a total of eight point units, varying the angle and height a little for each one.

5. Arrange and sew four point units, one A square and 4 C squares into three rows; press. Sew rows together to complete one Wonky Star block. Repeat to make a second block.

6. Layer a Wonky Star block and D square right sides together with a cotton batting square. Pin and stitch along one 8" side; trim batting close to seam.

7. Referring to Figure 4, flip block right side up with batting layer between the block and D square; press and topstitch ¼" from seam to make a pocket.

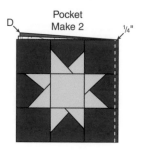

Figure 4

8. Repeat steps 6 and 7 to make a second pocket. Quilt each pocket in the ditch around the star points and echo-quilt a small square in the center of A.

9. Stitch E and F strips together on long sides to make a strip set as shown in Figure 5, starting with E and alternating color placement; press seams open.

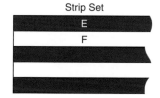

Figure 5

10. Place the backing rectangle right side down and cover with insulated batting, shiny side down, then cotton batting. Center strip set on top, right side up, and pin layers to secure. Quilt ¼" from the seams or as desired. Trim battings and backing even with top.

11. Referring to General Instructions on page 9, prepare two hanging loops from red tonal strips. Fold loops in half and pin raw ends to the back short ends of the quilted strip set, matching raw edges as shown in Figure 6; baste in place.

Figure 6

12. Referring to the Placement Diagram, place a pocket at each end of the quilted strip set with raw edges aligned and the topstitched edge toward the center of the strip set; pin or baste in place.

13. Referring to General Instructions on page 7, prepare binding and apply to raw edges to complete pot holder. ●

Here's a Tip

If you would like your potholder to be longer or shorter, alter the length of the red and white strips, backing and batting to make it custom fit for your table.

Stars & Stripes
Placement Diagram 27" x 8" excluding loops

Home Sweet Home

This house-shaped pot holder has appliquéd features and a few fun buttons for embellishment.

Skill Level
Beginner

Specifications
Pot Holder Size: 8" x 8" excluding loop

Materials

- Scraps turquoise, yellow and red tonals; coral floral and green print
- Small pieces black tonal and light-color print
- 1 (8") square cotton batting
- 1 (8") square needle-punched insulated batting
- Thread
- 3 (⅝") yellow flower-shape buttons
- 1 (⅜") black button
- Fusible web with paper release
- Basic sewing tools and supplies

Project Notes
Read all instructions before beginning this project.

Stitch right sides together using a ¼" seam allowance unless otherwise specified.

Refer to General Instructions on page 3 for specific construction and appliqué tips and techniques.

Cutting

From red tonal:
- Cut 1 (1¼" x 5") strip for hanging loop.

From black tonal:
- Cut 2 (3" x 8½") A rectangles.

From light-color print:
- Cut 2 (6" x 8½") B rectangles.

Completing the Pot Holder
Refer to the Placement Diagram and project photo throughout for positioning of pieces.

1. Sew A and B rectangles together on long edges to make an A-B unit as shown in Figure 1; repeat to make a second unit. Press seam on one unit toward A and seam on other unit toward B.

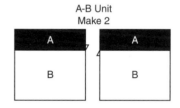

A-B Unit
Make 2

Figure 1

2. Center and baste edges of one A-B unit to cotton batting square for pot holder front.

3. Referring to Raw-Edge Fusible Appliqué on page 4, prepare appliqué templates using door window, door, window, curtain and bush patterns provided on the insert for this pot holder.

4. Trace appliqué shapes onto paper side of fusible web referring to list below for number to trace and cut out. Apply shapes to wrong side of fabric as listed below.

- Turquoise tonal: 1 door
- Yellow tonal: 1 each window and door window
- Coral floral: 1 curtain
- Green print: 1 bush

5. Cut out appliqué shapes and remove paper backing. Arrange appliqué shapes on the pot holder front as shown in Figure 2. Fuse in place.

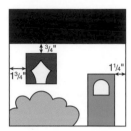

Figure 2

6. Machine blanket-stitch around each appliqué using matching thread.

7. Referring to Figure 3 to shape the roof, measure 2¼" in from each A top corner of the pot holder front and mark with a dot. Cut from the seam to the measured dot. Repeat with the second A-B unit to make pot holder back.

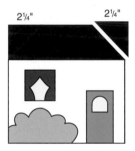

Figure 3

8. Referring to General Instructions on page 9, prepare the hanging loop. Fold loop in half and pin ends to left edge of roof, matching raw edges as shown in Figure 4. Baste to secure.

Figure 4

9. Center pot holder back, right side up, on the insulated batting square, shiny side up; place the pot holder front right sides together with the back, matching edges and seams. Pin layers to secure. Sew around edges, leaving a 3" opening on one side. Trim corners and turn right side out. Fold in seam allowance of opening and slip-stitch closed. Press edges flat and smooth.

10. Topstitch ¼" from outside edge and quilt by stitching around each appliqué.

11. Sew flower buttons on the bush and black button to the door for a doorknob to finish. ●

Home Sweet Home
Placement Diagram 8" x 8" excluding loop

Grandma's Fan

Grandma's Fan is a traditional quilt block that looks so sweet made up with vintage-style fabrics. A pair of them would make a wonderful Mother's Day gift.

Skill Level
Beginner

Specifications
Pot Holder Size: 7½" x 7½" excluding loop

Materials
- Scrap green berry print
- Small pieces of 2 floral/berry prints and 1 coordinating check
- Fat quarter yellow floral
- ⅛ yard red floral print
- 1 (7½" x 7½") square cotton batting
- 1 (7½" x 7½") square insulated batting
- Thread
- Fusible web with paper release
- Basic sewing tools and supplies

Project Notes
Read all instructions before beginning this project.

Stitch right sides together using a ¼" seam allowance unless otherwise specified.

Refer to General Instructions on page 3 for specific construction and appliqué tips and techniques.

Cutting
Prepare Dresden Blade template provided on insert.

From each floral/berry print & coordinating check:
- Cut 1 Dresden Blade.

From yellow floral:
- Cut 2 (7½") B squares and 1 (1¾" x 5") strip for hanging loop.

From red floral:
- Cut 1 (2½" by fabric width) binding strip.

Completing the Pot Holder
Refer to the Placement Diagram and project photo throughout for positioning of pieces.

1. Press ¼" to the wrong side on each side of the pointed end of each Dresden blade as shown in Figure 1.

Make 3

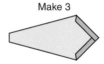

Figure 1

2. Join blades by seaming together on long sides with coordinating check blade in center to make the fan (Figure 2); press seams open.

Figure 2

3. Baste fan onto the right side of a B square with straight raw edges aligned as shown in Figure 3.

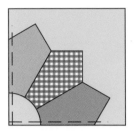

Figure 3

4. Referring to Raw-Edge Fusible Appliqué on page 4, prepare quarter-circle center appliqué template and trace appliqué shape onto paper side of fusible web referring to list below for number to trace and cut out. Apply shape to wrong side of fabric as listed below.

• Green print: 1 quarter-circle center

5. Cut out appliqué shape prepared in step 4 and remove paper backing. Arrange quarter-circle center appliqué on corner of B square, covering curved raw edge of the fan. Fuse in place.

6. Pin fused B square to the cotton batting square. Machine blanket-stitch around blade tips and curved edge of quarter-circle center using matching thread to complete the pot holder front.

7. Layer remaining B square, wrong side down; insulated batting, shiny side down, and pot holder front, right side up; pin to hold. Stitch ¼" from edges on the inside of each petal and echo-quilt on the B section beginning ½" from the edge of the fan.

8. Referring to General Instructions on page 9, prepare the hanging loop. Fold loop in half and pin ends to adjacent sides of pot holder back at corner as shown in Figure 4. Baste to secure.

3/4"
3/4"

Figure 4

9. Referring to General Instructions on page 7, prepare binding and apply to the raw edges to finish. ●

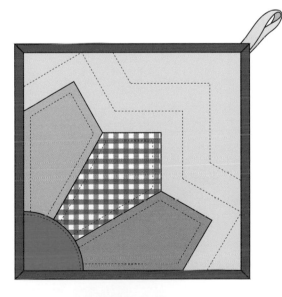

Grandma's Fan
Placement Diagram 7½" x 7½"
excluding loop

Apple Harvest

A nice, crisp apple just pulled off the tree is a tasty treat indeed! This pot holder has pockets on each side to slip your fingers and thumb into for a good grip.

Skill Level
Beginner

Specifications
Pot Holder Size: 8½" x 8¼" excluding loop

Materials
- Scrap brown dot
- Fat quarter each red tonal, white-with-gold/red dots and green dot
- Cotton batting
- 1 (9") square needle-punched insulated batting
- Thread
- Green pearl cotton No. 8 or 12, or embroidery floss
- Basic sewing tools and supplies

Project Notes
Read all instructions before beginning this project.

Stitch right sides together using a ¼" seam allowance unless otherwise specified.

Refer to General Instructions on page 3 for specific construction and appliqué tips and techniques.

Cutting
Prepare templates for apple and left and right pockets using patterns provided on insert.

From brown dot:
- Cut 1 (1¾" x 5") strip for hanging loops.

From red tonal & white-with-gold/red dots:
- Using prepared templates, cut 1 apple shape and 2 pocket shapes from each fabric.

From green dot:
- Cut 2½"-wide bias strips to measure 60" when joined for binding.

From cotton batting:
- Cut 1 apple shape and 2 pocket shapes using prepared templates.
- Cut 1 (3" x 4½") rectangle.

From insulated batting:
- Cut 1 apple shape using prepared template.

Completing the Pot Holder
Refer to the Placement Diagram and project photo throughout for positioning of pieces.

1. To make pockets, layer one each red tonal and white-with-gold/red dots pocket shape with wrong sides together; place a cotton batting pocket between the fabric layers. Baste to hold. Repeat to make a second layered pocket.

2. Referring to General Instructions on page 7, prepare bias binding and apply to inner edge of each layered pocket.

3. Layer the apple shapes as follows: red tonal, right side down; insulated batting, shiny side down; cotton batting; and white-with-gold/red dots, right side up. Baste edges to hold and quilt apple core shape in the center.

4. Referring to General Instructions on page 9, prepare hanging loop. Fold loop in half and pin to top center on back of quilted apple as shown in Figure 1. Baste to secure.

Figure 1

5. Referring to Figure 2, position pockets on front of quilted apple, matching top, side and bottom edges and baste to hold.

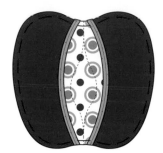

Figure 2

6. Referring to General Instructions on page 7, bind outer edges of apple.

7. Make leaf template using pattern provided on insert. Referring to Padded Appliqué on page 6, prepare one leaf from green dot, using the 3½" x 4" cotton batting rectangle and making a 1" slash for turning.

8. Place leaf at the top of the right-hand pocket. Using 1 strand of pearl cotton or 2 strands of embroidery floss and a running stitch, sew along the center of the leaf, being careful to stitch into pocket only to finish. ●

Running Stitch

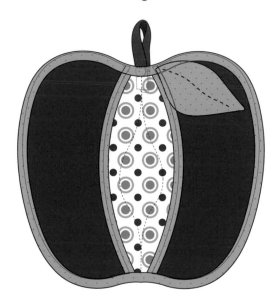

Apple Harvest
Placement Diagram 8½" x 8¼"
excluding loop

Falling Leaves

One of the most beautiful sights of autumn is the colorful leaves falling from the trees. To make this pot holder, sew strips of a variety of red prints together. When you cut the pieced units on the diagonal, you'll have enough to make two pot holders. Try this one in all the colors of fall!

Skill Level
Beginner

Specifications
Pot Holder Size: 8¼" x 9½" excluding loop

Materials
Materials listed are for two pot holders.

- Scraps of 18–20 red strips at least 9½" long and varying in width from 1¼"–1¾" for A
- Fat quarter each gold and red tonal
- 1 (10" x 20") rectangle cotton batting
- 1 (10" x 20") rectangle needle-punched insulated batting
- Thread
- Basic sewing tools and supplies

Project Notes
Read all instructions before beginning this project.

Stitch right sides together using a ¼" seam allowance unless otherwise specified.

Refer to General Instructions on page 3 for specific construction and appliqué tips and techniques.

Cutting
Prepare leaf template using pattern provided on insert.

From gold tonal:
- Cut 2 (1¾" x 5") strips for hanging loops.
- Cut 2½"-wide bias strips to measure 60" when joined for binding.

From red tonal:
- Cut 2 leaf shapes for backing using prepared template.

From each batting:
- Cut 2 leaf shapes.

Completing the Pot Holders
Refer to the Placement Diagram and project photo throughout for positioning of pieces.

1. Join A strips on long sides to make a strip set at least 9½" x 19"; press seams open. Cut into two 9½" squares.

2. Cut one pieced square on the diagonal from the upper left corner to the lower right corner to make two pieced triangles as shown in Figure 1a.

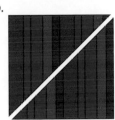

a.   b.

Figure 1

3. Referring to Figure 1b, cut the second pieced square on the diagonal from the lower left corner to the upper right corner to make two reversed pieced triangles.

4. Sew a pieced triangle to a reversed pieced triangle on the diagonal edge to make a square unit as shown in Figure 2; press seam open. Repeat with remaining set of triangles to make a second square unit.

Square Unit
Make 2

Figure 2

5. Use the leaf template to cut a leaf shape from each square unit, aligning the seam of the unit with the seam line on the template.

6. Referring to General Instructions on page 9, prepare two hanging loops and two 30"-long bias binding strips.

7. Fold hanging loops in half and pin to top front of each leaf backing as shown in Figure 3. Baste to secure.

Figure 3

8. Layer each leaf as follows: leaf backing, right side down; insulated batting, shiny side down; cotton batting; and leaf front, right side up. Baste edges to hold and quilt along the center seam and with several curved vein lines from the center outward.

9. Referring to General Instructions on page 7, bind outer edges of each leaf to finish. ●

Falling Leaves
Placement Diagram 8¹⁄₄" x 9¹⁄₂"
excluding loop

Scaredy-Cat

No tricks, just treats when you make this black cat pot holder.
Or omit the Halloween colors and make a cat that looks like yours!

Skill Level
Beginner

Specifications
Pot Holder Size: 7½" x 8½" excluding tail and bow

Materials
- Scrap of orange-with-black dot
- Fat quarter black tonal
- 1 each 8" x 9" and 2½" x 6" rectangle cotton batting
- 1 (8" x 9") rectangle needle-punched insulated batting
- 2 (⅜") green buttons
- 1 (⅜") black button
- 1 (⅞") green spider button
- 1 (¾") plastic ring
- Thread
- Basic sewing tools and supplies

Project Notes
Read all instructions before beginning this project.

Stitch right sides together using a ¼" seam allowance unless otherwise specified.

Refer to General Instructions on page 3 for specific construction and appliqué tips and techniques.

Cutting
Prepare cat template using pattern provided on insert.

From orange-with-black dot:
- Cut 1 (2½" x 18") strip for bow.

From black tonal:
- Cut 2 cat shapes for front and backing using prepared template.

From each batting:
- Cut 1 cat shape using prepared template.

Completing the Pot Holder
Refer to the Placement Diagram and project photo throughout for positioning of pieces.

1. Make tail template using pattern provided on insert. Referring to Padded Appliqué on page 6, prepare tail from black tonal, using 2½" x 6" cotton batting rectangle and leaving straight edge open for turning.

2. Topstitch ¼" from long edges of tail.

3. Layer the cat pieces as follows: cotton batting; insulated batting, shiny side up; cat backing, right side up; and cat front, right side down. Pin layers to secure. Sew around edges, leaving an opening where indicated on pattern. To reduce bulk, trim insulated batting close to seam. Clip curves and turn right side out. Press edges flat and smooth.

4. Fold in seam allowance of opening and slip ¼" of open end of tail inside. Slip-stitch opening closed catching tail in the stitches.

5. Topstitch ¼" from outside edge of cat shape. Quilt whiskers in face as shown in Figure 1 and stitch curved line for neck.

Figure 1

6. To make bow, fold orange strip in half lengthwise with right sides together. Referring to Figure 2, sew the short and long raw edges together, leaving a 2" opening in the middle.

Figure 2

7. Trim the corners and turn right side out, press. Fold in the seam allowance on the opening and slipstitch edges together to close.

8. Tie fabric strip in a bow and tack the knot to the left end of the quilted neck line.

9. Sew green buttons to face for eyes, black button over center of whiskers for nose and spider to one tail of bow.

10. Referring to General Instructions on page 9, sew plastic ring to back of right ear to finish. ●

Scaredy-Cat
Placement Diagram 7½" x 8½"
excluding tail & bow

Turkey Day

There's always lots of cooking going on for Thanksgiving so this pot holder will definitely come in handy. The turkey body is pieced like the traditional Bear Paw quilt block. Make it in fall colors for Traditional Tom or be inspired by the color option shown for Trendy Tom!

Skill Level
Beginner

Specifications
Pot Holder Size: 8" x 8" excluding loop

Materials
- Scraps dark brown, medium brown, rust, gold, dark gold and red tonals and cream-with-mulitcolored dots
- ⅛ yard multicolored stripe
- 1 (8") square backing fabric
- 1 (8") square cotton batting
- 1 (8") square needle-punched insulated batting
- 1 (⁵⁄₁₆") black button
- Thread
- Basic sewing tools and supplies

Project Notes
Read all instructions before beginning this project.

Stitch right sides together using a ¼" seam allowance unless otherwise specified.

Refer to General Instructions on page 3 for specific construction and appliqué tips and techniques.

Cutting

From dark brown tonal:
- Cut 1 (5½") E square.

From rust tonal:
- Cut 1 (3½") B square.

From gold tonal:
- Cut 1 (3½") C square.

From cream-with-multicolored dots:
- Cut 2 (3½") A squares and 1 (3") D square and 1 (1¼" x 5") strip for hanging loop.

From multicolored stripe:
- Cut 1 (2½" by fabric width) binding strip.

Completing the Pot Holder
Refer to the Placement Diagram and project photo throughout for positioning of pieces.

1. Draw a diagonal line from corner to corner on the wrong side of each A square.

2. Referring to Figure 1, pair one each A and B square right sides together and stitch ¼" on each side of drawn line. Cut on drawn line to make two A-B units; press. Trim each unit to 3" square, keeping seam centered.

Figure 1

3. Repeat step 2 using one each A and C square to make two A-C units.

4. Arrange and stitch A-B and A-C units with D square to make two pieced strips as shown in Figure 2; press.

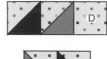

Figure 2

5. Referring to Figure 3, stitch the shorter pieced strip to one side of E square; press toward E.

Figure 3

6. Sew longer pieced strip to top of E unit as shown in Figure 4 to complete the pieced front unit.

Figure 4

7. Center and baste pieced front unit to cotton batting square.

8. Referring to Raw-Edge Fusible Appliqué on page 4, prepare appliqué templates using turkey body, wattle and beak patterns provided on the insert for this pot holder.

9. Trace appliqué shapes onto paper side of fusible web referring to list below for number to trace and cut out. Apply shapes to wrong side of fabric as listed below.

- Medium brown tonal: 1 turkey body
- Red tonal: 1 wattle
- Dark gold tonal: 1 beak

10. Cut out appliqué shapes and remove paper backing. Arrange appliqués on pieced front unit with bottom of turkey 2½" up from bottom corner as shown in Figure 5. Fuse in place.

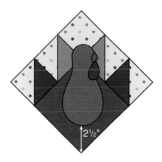

Figure 5

11. Machine blanket-stitch around each appliqué using matching thread to complete the pot holder front.

12. Layer pot holder front and backing square, wrong sides together with insulated batting between; pin layers to secure. Quilt in the ditch on the patchwork and around each appliqué.

13. Referring to General Instructions on page 9, prepare hanging loop. Fold loop in half and pin raw edges on adjacent sides of the top corner of the pot holder back as shown in Figure 6. Baste to secure.

Figure 6

14. Referring to General Instructions on page 7, prepare binding and apply to edges.

15. Sew black button to head for eye to finish. ●

Turkey Day
Placement Diagram 8" x 8"
excluding loop

Gingerbread House

All adorned with mounds of frosting and little candies,
this gingerbread house is ready to decorate your kitchen!

Skill Level
Beginner

Specifications
Pot Holder Size: 8½" x 8½"

Materials
- Scraps red dot and white, green, red and brown tonals
- Fat quarter blue snowflake print
- ⅛ yard red tonal
- 1 (8½") square cotton batting
- 1 (8½") square needle-punched insulated batting
- Thread
- 4 (⅝") green buttons
- 2 (⅝") red buttons
- 1 (⁷⁄₁₆") white button
- 1 (⅝") white snowflake button
- 2 (¾") plastic rings
- Fusible web with paper release
- Basic sewing tools and supplies

Project Notes
Read all instructions before beginning this project.

Stitch right sides together using a ¼" seam allowance unless otherwise specified.

Refer to General Instructions on page 3 for specific construction and appliqué tips and techniques.

Cutting

From blue snowflake print:
- Cut 2 (8½") A squares.

From red tonal:
- Cut 1 (2½" by fabric width) strip for binding.

Completing the Pot Holder
Refer to the Placement Diagram and project photo throughout for positioning of pieces.

1. Baste cotton batting square to wrong side of one A square for pot holder front.

Here's a Tip
Apply white medium-weight fusible interfacing to the wrong side of the white tonal before adding fusible web to prevent shadowing of dark colors.

2. Referring to Raw-Edge Fusible Appliqué on page 4, prepare appliqué templates using door, roof snow, chimney snow, tree, chimney, heart and house patterns provided on the insert for this pot holder.

3. Trace appliqué shapes onto paper side of fusible web referring to list below for number to trace and cut out. Apply shapes to wrong side of fabric as listed below.

- Red dot: 1 door
- White tonal: 1 each roof snow and chimney snow
- Green tonal: 1 tree
- Red tonal: 1 each chimney and heart
- Brown tonal: 1 house

4. Cut out appliqué shapes and remove paper backing. Arrange appliqués on the pot holder front referring to Figure 1 for order of placement. Center house ¾" up from bottom edge and place bottom edges of tree and door even with bottom edge of house. Fuse in place.

Figure 1

5. Machine blanket-stitch around each appliqué using matching thread.

6. Layer pot holder front and remaining A square backing wrong sides together; place the insulated batting square, shiny side down, in between front and backing. Pin layers to secure. Quilt around the appliqués or as desired.

7. Referring to General Instructions on page 7, prepare binding and apply to the edges.

8. Sew green and red buttons to the roof snow, the white button to the door for a doorknob and the snowflake button to the top of the tree.

9. Referring to General Instructions on page 9, sew a plastic ring to each top back corner of pot holder to finish. ●

Gingerbread House
Placement Diagram 8½" x 8½"

Gingerbread Boy

This little guy is all ready to help you pull those hot gingerbread cookies out of the oven! He has rickrack frosting, a bow tie and little buttons for embellishment.

Skill Level
Beginner

Specifications
Pot Holder Size: 8½" x 8½"

Materials
- Scraps brown tonal, red mini dot and green-with-multicolored dots
- Fat quarter blue tonal
- ⅛ yard red tonal
- 1 (8½") square cotton batting
- 1 (8½") square needle-punched insulated batting
- Thread
- White pearl cotton No. 8 or 12, or embroidery floss
- 6" length of ¼" white rickrack
- 2 (³⁄₁₆") black buttons
- 2 (³⁄₁₆") red buttons
- 1 (⅜") red button
- 2 (¾") plastic rings
- Seam sealant
- Fusible web with paper release
- Basic sewing tools and supplies

Project Notes
Read all instructions before beginning this project.

Stitch right sides together using a ¼" seam allowance unless otherwise specified.

Refer to General Instructions on page 3 for specific construction and appliqué tips and techniques.

Cutting

From red mini dot:
- Cut 1 (2½" x 3") B rectangle for bow tie.

From blue tonal:
- Cut 2 (8½") A squares.

From red tonal:
- Cut 1 (2½" by fabric width) strip for binding.

Completing the Pot Holder
Refer to the Placement Diagram and project photo throughout for positioning of pieces.

1. Baste cotton batting square to wrong side of one A square for the pot holder front.

2. Referring to Raw-Edge Fusible Appliqué on page 4, prepare appliqué templates using boy and vest patterns provided on the insert for this pot holder.

3. Trace appliqué shapes onto paper side of fusible web referring to list below for number to trace and cut out. Apply shapes to wrong side of fabric as listed below.

- Brown tonal: 1 boy
- Green-with-multicolored dots: 1 vest

4. Cut out appliqué shapes and remove paper backing. Arrange appliqués on the pot holder front, centering the boy piece on the square. Fuse in place.

5. Machine blanket-stitch around each appliqué using matching thread.

6. Cut rickrack into four equal pieces and apply seam sealant to one end of each piece. Position a piece on an arm and trim unsealed end to fit exactly. Apply seam sealant to trimmed end. Hand-stitch points of rickrack in place. Repeat for remaining arm and both legs.

7. Transfer the smile to the boy's head and backstitch on the line using 1 strand of pearl cotton or 2 strands of embroidery floss.

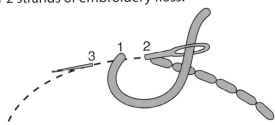

Backstitch

8. Layer pot holder front and remaining A square for backing wrong sides together; place the insulated batting square, shiny side down between front and backing. Pin layers to secure. Quilt around the appliqués or as desired.

9. Referring to General Instructions on page 7, prepare binding and apply to the edges.

10. To make the bow tie, fold the B rectangle in half lengthwise with right sides together; stitch all around the raw edges, leaving a 1" opening on the long edge as shown in Figure 1. Trim corners and turn right side out. Press and fold in seam

allowance on opening. Slip-stitch edges together on opening to close.

Figure 1

11. Using doubled and knotted red thread, sew a small gathering stitch down the center of the B strip as shown in Figure 2a. Pull thread to gather center tightly and wrap thread around strip several times before knotting (Figure 2b).

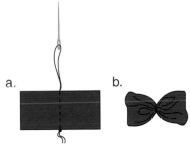

Figure 2

12. Sew ⅜" red button to center of bow tie and then to neck of boy appliqué.

13. Sew black buttons to face for eyes and ³⁄₁₆" red buttons to ends of smile.

14. Referring to General Instructions on page 9, sew a plastic ring to each top back corner of pot holder to finish. ●

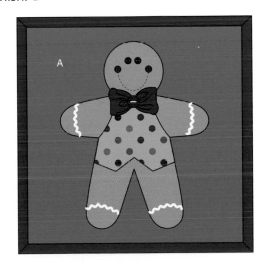

Gingerbread Boy
Placement Diagram 8½" x 8½"

Christmas Star

This pot holder is based on a traditional quilt block in holiday colors. Star blocks are great favorites, so try it in other color combinations too.

Skill Level

Beginner

Specifications

Pot Holder Size: 8½" x 8½" excluding loop

Materials

- Scraps red and green tonals
- Fat quarter black holly print
- ⅛ yard red-and-green stripe
- 1 (8½") square cotton batting
- 1 (8½") square needle-punched insulated batting
- Thread
- 1 (¾") red 2-hole button
- 1 (⅝") green 2-hole button
- Fusible web with paper release
- Basic sewing tools and supplies

Project Notes

Read all instructions before beginning this project.

Stitch right sides together using a ¼" seam allowance unless otherwise specified.

Refer to General Instructions on page 3 for specific construction and appliqué tips and techniques.

Cutting

From red tonal:

- Cut 4 (3") B squares and 1 (1¾" x 5") strip for hanging loop.

From green tonal:

- Cut 4 (3") D squares.

From black holly print:

- Cut 4 (2½") A squares, 4 (3") C squares and 1 (8½") backing square.

From red-and-green stripe:

- Cut 1 (2½" by fabric width) strip for binding.

Completing the Pot Holder

Refer to the Block Diagram and project photo throughout for positioning of pieces.

1. Pair two each B and C squares, two each B and D squares, and two each C and D squares. Draw a diagonal line from corner to corner on the wrong side of the lighter square in each pair.

2. Referring to Figure 1, place a B square right sides together with a C square; stitch ¼" on each side of drawn line. Cut on drawn line to make two B-C units; press seam toward darker triangle. Repeat to make a total of four B-C units.

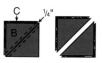

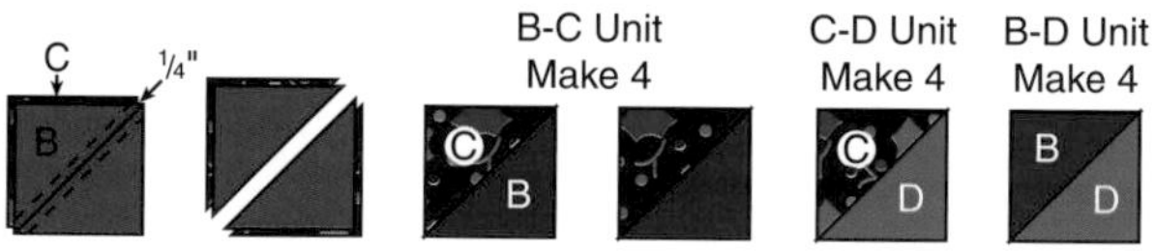

B-C Unit Make 4 **C-D Unit Make 4** **B-D Unit Make 4**

Figure 1

3. Repeat step 2 with B/D and C/D pairs to make four each B-D and C-D units, again referring to Figure 1.

4. Arrange and sew A squares and pieced units into four rows. Sew the rows together to complete the pot holder front.

5. Layer as follows: backing square, right side down; insulated batting square, shiny side down; cotton batting square and pot holder front, right side up. Baste layers to secure. Quilt ¼" from each seam or as desired.

6. Referring to General Instructions on page 9, prepare hanging loop. Fold loop in half and pin raw edges to adjacent sides of one back corner as shown in Figure 2. Baste in place.

¾" ¾"

Figure 2

7. Referring to General Instructions on page 7, prepare binding and apply to the edges.

8. Stack the two buttons with the smaller on top and sew to the center of the star to finish. ●

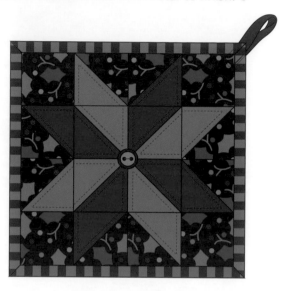

Christmas Star
Placement Diagram 8½" x 8½"
excluding loop

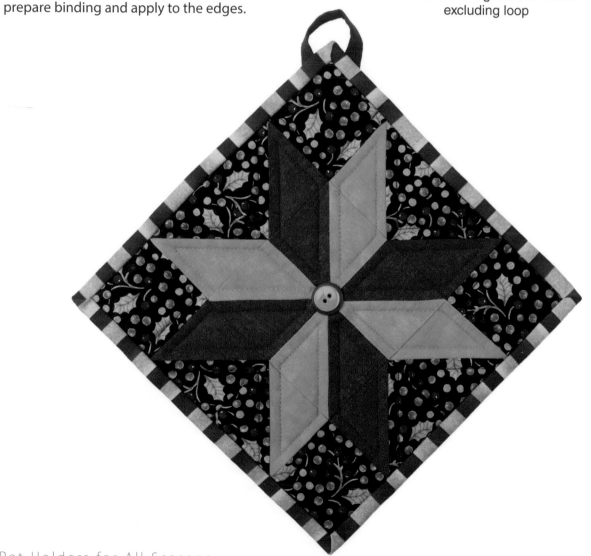

Happy Snowman

This cheerful fellow can decorate your kitchen all winter long.
He has an appliquéd nose, dimensional embellishments
and a little embroidery to give him that happy face.

Skill Level
Beginner

Specifications
Pot Holder Size: 8" x 8" excluding bow and leaf

Materials
- Scraps green and orange tonals
- Fat eighth each white and black tonals, and red-with-multicolored dots
- Cotton batting
- 1 (8½") square needle-punched insulated batting
- Thread
- 2 (1¹¹⁄₁₆") black buttons
- 1 (⅝") red button
- Black and pink pearl cotton No. 8 or 12, or embroidery floss
- 2 (¾") plastic rings
- Fusible web with paper release
- Basic sewing tools and supplies

Project Notes
Read all instructions before beginning this project.

Stitch right sides together using a ¼" seam allowance unless otherwise specified.

Refer to General Instructions on page 3 for specific construction and appliqué tips and techniques.

Cutting

From white tonal:
- Cut 2 (4½" x 8½") B rectangles.

From black tonal:
- Cut 2 (3½" x 8½") A rectangles and 2 (1½" x 10½") D strips.

From red-with-multicolored dots:
- Cut 1 (3" x 8½") strip for scarf tie and 2 (1½" x 8½") C rectangles.

From cotton batting:
- Cut 1 (8½") square, 1 (1½" x 10½") strip and 1 (3" x 4") rectangle.

Completing the Pot Holder

Refer to the Placement Diagram and project photo throughout for positioning of pieces.

1. Referring to Figure 1, join A, B and C rectangles to make pot holder front; repeat to make pot holder back. Press seams on one unit toward B and seams on other unit away from B.

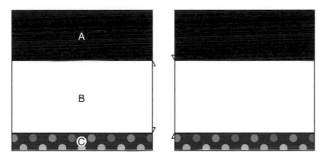

Figure 1

2. Baste cotton batting square to wrong side of pot holder front.

3. Referring to Raw-Edge Fusible Appliqué on page 4, prepare appliqué templates using nose pattern provided on the insert for this pot holder.

4. Trace appliqué shapes onto paper side of fusible web referring to list below for number to trace and cut out. Apply shapes to wrong side of fabric as listed below.

• Orange tonal: 1 nose

5. Cut out appliqué shape and remove paper backing. Arrange nose on the pot holder front referring to Figure 2. Fuse in place.

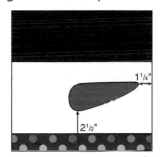

Figure 2

6. Machine blanket-stitch around nose using matching thread.

7. Transfer smile and two cheeks embroidery designs to pot holder front. Use 1 strand of pearl cotton or 2 strands of embroidery floss and a running stitch to embroider smile with black and cheeks with pink.

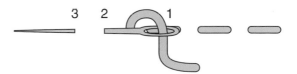

Running Stitch

8. Layer pot holder pieces in the following order: insulated batting, shiny side up; pot holder back, right side up; and pot holder front, right side down. Pin layers to secure. Sew around edges, leaving a 3½" opening in one side. To reduce bulk, trim insulated batting close to seam. Clip curves and turn right side out. Fold in seam allowance of opening and slip-stitch closed. Press edges flat and smooth.

9. Topstitch ¼" from outside edge and quilt around nose appliqué.

10. To make hat brim, place D strips right sides together on the same-size cotton batting strip; pin to hold. Sew around edges, leaving a 3" opening in one side. To reduce bulk, trim batting close to seam and clip corners. Turn right side out. Fold in seam allowance of opening and slip-stitch closed. Press edges flat and smooth.

11. Topstitch ¼" from outside edge of brim.

12. Center hat brim on snowman front 2" down from top as shown in Figure 3. Sew on the previous topstitching where the brim overlaps the pot holder.

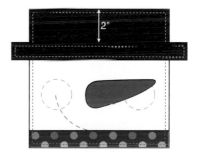

Figure 3

13. Make holly leaf template using pattern provided on insert. Referring to Padded Appliqué on page 6, prepare one holly leaf from green tonal, using the 3" x 4" cotton batting rectangle and making a 1" slash for turning.

14. Quilt leaf vein lines with green thread.

15. Position holly leaf on hat referring to the Placement Diagram. Stitch over center vein line to attach.

16. To make the scarf tie, fold red strip in half lengthwise with right sides together and sew along the short and long ends, leaving a 2" opening on one long side. Trim corners and turn right side out; press. Fold in seam allowance on opening and slip-stitch edges together to close. Tie a knot in the center and tack the knot to the right end of the bottom scarf piece.

17. Sew black buttons to the face for eyes and red button to the end of the holly leaf for a berry.

18. Referring to the General Instructions on page 9, sew a plastic ring to the back of each top corner to finish. ●

Happy Snowman
Placement Diagram 8" x 8"
excluding bow & leaf

Microwave Bowl Cozy

Cold weather calls for hot soup and this unique pot holder is "souper" for heating foods in the microwave. Set the bowl inside the pot holder cozy and put it in the microwave. When food is hot, you can grasp the corners of the pot holder to lift it out.

Skill Level
Beginner

Specifications
Pot Holder Size: 5½" x 5½" x 2¼" excluding corner handles

Materials
- Fat quarter each dark gray floral and light gray word print
- ¼ yard yellow tonal
- 2 (10") squares cotton batting
- Thread
- Basic sewing tools and supplies

Project Notes
Read all instructions before beginning this project.

Stitch right sides together using a ¼" seam allowance unless otherwise specified.

Refer to General Instructions on page 3 for specific construction and appliqué tips and techniques.

Cutting

From each fat quarter:
- Cut 1 (10") A square.

From yellow tonal:
- Cut 2 (2½" by fabric width) binding strips.

Completing the Cozy
Refer to the Placement Diagram and project photo throughout for positioning of pieces.

1. Layer the two A squares wrong sides together with both cotton batting squares between. Baste to hold. Referring to Figure 1, quilt a square 1¼" from the outside edge and two more squares 1" apart inside the first. Quilt an X from corner to corner.

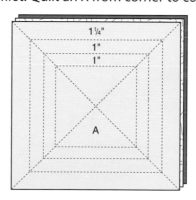

Figure 1

2. Referring to General Instructions on page 7, prepare binding and apply to edges of quilted square.

3. To form the bowl shape, fold two sides together at a corner with the dark gray on the outside. Draw a line 2¼" from the binding down to the fold at a right angle. Stitch on this line, backstitching at beginning and end as shown in Figure 2. Repeat on remaining three corners.

Figure 2

4. Referring to Figure 3, flatten the inner edges of a corner to make a handle. Stitch across the flattened section through all layers to secure, backstitching at beginning and end. Repeat on remaining three corners to complete the cozy. ●

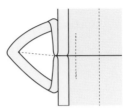

Figure 3

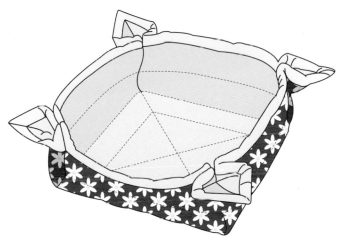

Microwave Bowl Cozy
Placement Diagram 5½" x 5½" x 2¼"
excluding corner handles

Annie's® *Pot Holders for All Seasons* is published by Annie's, 306 East Parr Road, Berne, IN 46711. Printed in USA. Copyright © 2016, 2020 Annie's. All rights reserved. This publication may not be reproduced in part or in whole without written permission from the publisher.

RETAIL STORES: If you would like to carry this publication or any other Annie's publications, visit AnniesWSL.com.

Every effort has been made to ensure that the instructions in this publication are complete and accurate. We cannot, however, take responsibility for human error, typographical mistakes or variations in individual work. Please visit AnniesCustomerService.com to check for pattern updates.

ISBN: 978-1-59012-670-7   Library of Congress Control Number: 2016953703   15